Devis

The Mother Goddesses

Om KIDZ
An imprint of Om Books International

First Published in 2024 by

Om Kidz | Om Books International

Corporate & Editorial Office
A-12, Sector 64, Noida 201 301
Uttar Pradesh, India
Phone: +91 120 477 4100
Email: editorial@ombooks.com
Website: www.ombooksinternational.com

Sales Office
107, Ansari Road, Darya Ganj
New Delhi 110 002, India
Phone: +91 11 4000 9000
Email: sales@ombooks.com

ISBN: 978-93-53769-53-6

Printed in India

10 9 8 7 6 5 4 3 2 1

Contents

Durga and Mahisha

Mahisha was a very evil and fierce demon. He performed a severe penance to please Lord Brahma. When Lord Brahma finally appeared before him, Mahisha said, “Lord, please grant me immortality.”

"Everyone who is born has to die. You cannot be granted immortality. Choose any other boon and I will be pleased to grant it," said Lord Brahma.

Mahisha thought for a moment. Then he came up with a clever boon. "If I have to die, let it be at the hands of a woman," he said. "So be it," said Brahma and disappeared. "How can any woman overpower my strength and valour," thought Mahisha, and rejoiced that he had almost become immortal.

His evil designs knew no bounds. He gathered his army of demons and marched to Amaravati, capital of the gods. "Charge!" roared Mahisha. "Your attempts to subdue Amaravati have always been foiled," said Indra. "But this time, I will not be defeated," said Mahisha and charged at the gods.

A fierce battle took place between the gods and the demons. And as Mahisha predicted, the gods were driven out of the heavens by the demons. Mahisha sat on Indra's throne and ruled over all the three worlds. The demons continued with their evil ways by destroying the penance of the sages. They tormented the people on Earth who would pray to any god. "Mahisha is the only god you should

know," they shouted and hit the people praying in the temples.

Unable to bear Mahisha and his army's ways, everyone rushed to Mount Kailash, the abode of Lord Shiva. "Lord, only you can save us from the evil demon Mahisha," pleaded the gods. Brahma and Vishnu were also present at Kailash, hearing the desperate pleas of the gods.

Suddenly, there was a flash

of light from all the three of them. The light joined to produce a lady seated on a ferocious lion. "Rise, Mother Durga!" said Lord Shiva. "She will free you from the torments of the demons," said Lord Vishnu.

"Oh Goddess, your arrival brings us a new hope," said the gods welcoming Goddess Durga. Shiva created a trident from his own and gifted it to her. Similarly, Lord Vishnu created another discus and gifted it to

her. Indra gave her the thunderbolt and Brahma gifted her a necklace with sacred beads. Armed with her new weapons, Durga charged ahead. "Mahisha, I will find you wherever you are and kill you," roared Durga.

Seated on her vehicle – the lion – Durga charged towards Mahisha's palace. The mountains shook and the seas trembled as she travelled. Mahisha saw the sudden change in the environment and was alarmed. "What is happening," he wondered as trees collapsed in front of him.

He rushed to the entrance of his palace, to find Durga waiting for him. "Here is the form of death you desired," said Goddess Durga. "You are just a woman," said Mahisha without any fright. "Make no mistake," she replied. "I am the boon that you asked Lord Brahma for," said Durga. "Prepare to fight," she roared.

Mahisha and Durga fought a bitter battle. Durga breathed out furiously, and from her breath arose thousands of warriors. They charged at Mahisha's army.

Mahisha was furious. "I will kill her and her army," he screamed and charged at her turning into a buffalo. Durga threw her noose around his neck and pulled him. He quickly changed into a lion, but Durga chopped off the lion's head. Mahisha then assumed

his original form for a few moments, before he turned himself into a wild elephant and charged at Durga. But the goddess was very quick, and chopped off the elephant's trunk. Seething with fury, Mahisha again assumed the form of a wild buffalo. But this time,

Durga jumped from her lion on to the buffalo's body and trampled Mahisha with her foot. Mahisha's body emerged in half from the buffalo, but Durga killed him with her trident.

Finally, the evil demon was no more! "Goddess Durga, you are the destroyer of evil and the protector of all the gods and mankind. Always shower us with your blessings," said the gods rejoicing over Mahisha's death.

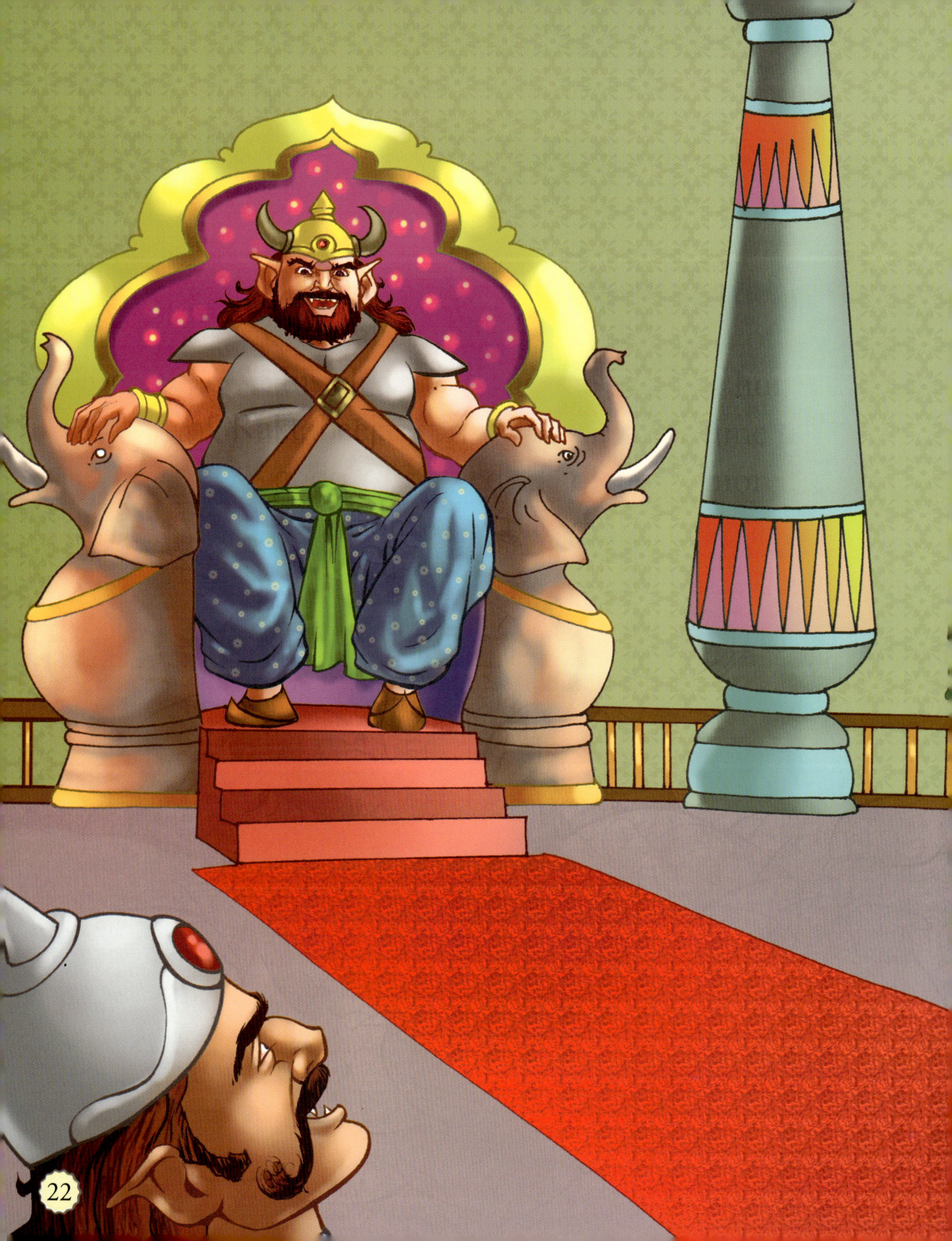

Kali

Heaven had been seized by the demons. Lord Indra, the King of the gods, had been driven out of his kingdom once again.

There was darkness and terror everywhere. The ruler of the demons—Shumbha—had vowed never to let the gods enter Heaven again.

When the battle between the demons and the gods had ended, a few demons saw the gods running towards a mountain. "Let us find out their hiding place," said Chanda, a companion to Munda, another demon. Chanda and Munda followed the gods to the sacred mountain, Himavat, where the Gods were praying to the Mother Goddess. "Oh Mother Goddess, please save us from

Shumbha. With his evil ways, we have been driven out of Heaven. Please bring back peace to the three worlds," pleaded the gods.

Chanda and Munda were watching this from the bushes nearby. Goddess Parvati, the wife of Lord

Shiva, was passing by. She heard the pleas of the gods and decided to help them. From her body emerged Goddess Ambika. "Oh beautiful goddess, we plead with you to destroy the evil demons," said the gods.

"Let us inform our King Shumbha right away," said Chanda to Munda, and they both rushed back to the palace. "Lord, we have seen a beautiful lady being worshipped by the gods," said Chanda. "Is she very beautiful?" asked Shumbha. "She is the most beautiful lady we have ever seen," said Munda. "If that is true,

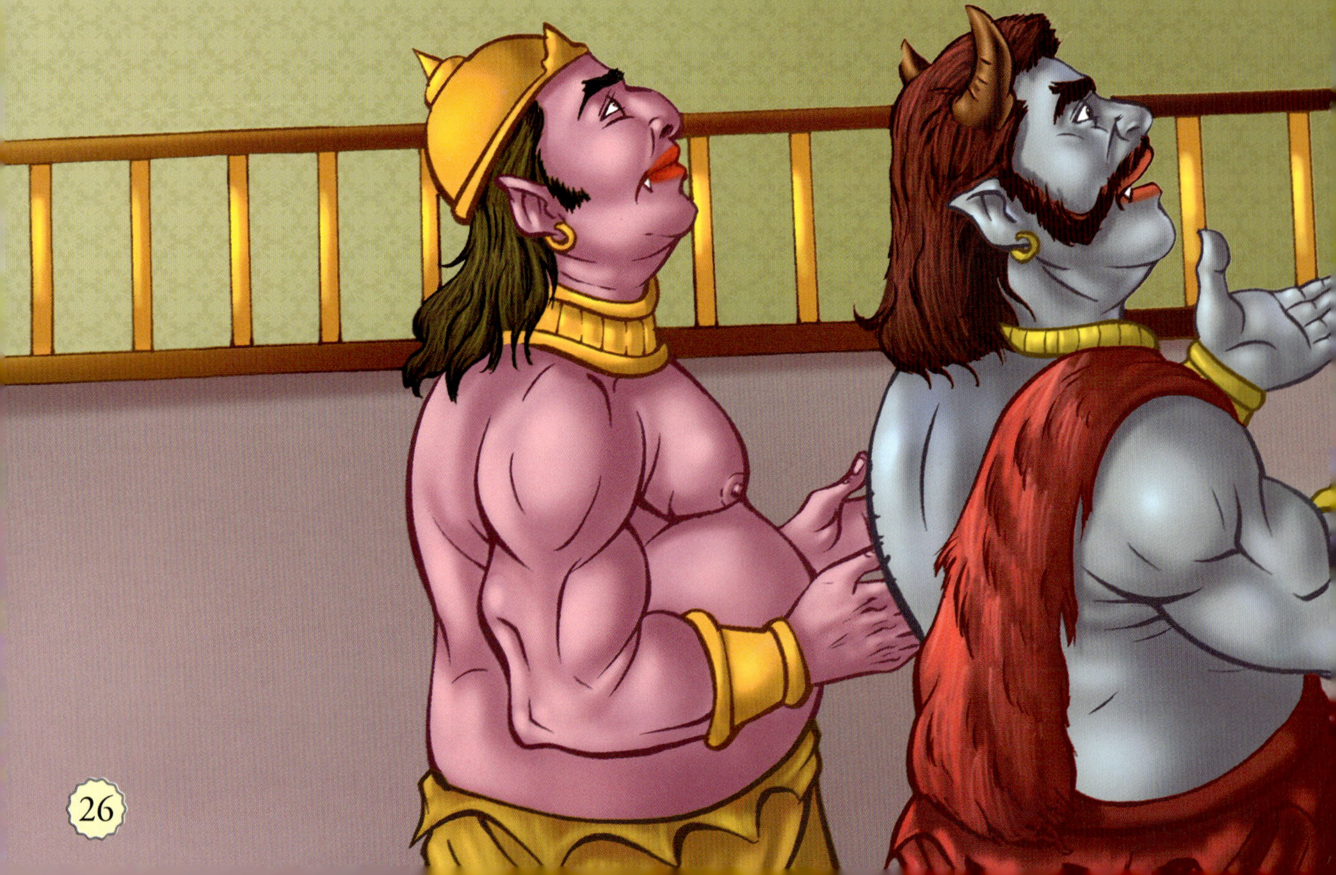

please bring her to me, I want her to be my wife," said Shumbha.

Chanda and Munda went back to Mount Himavat, where they had seen the beautiful goddess. "There she is," shouted Chanda. "Oh beautiful lady, the lord of the three worlds—Shumbha—wishes to make you his wife. We are here to take you

with us," said Chanda.

"If he desires to wed me, he must defeat me in a battle," said the goddess.

Chanda and Munda carried the news back to Shumbha. "I will send my most trusted commander,

Dhumralochana, to bring her to me," said Shumbha and summoned him. "Dhumralochana, bring Ambika to me now!" ordered Shumbha.

Dhumralochana went to fight Ambika with his army. As he ran to seize her, Ambika let out a deep sigh. Within seconds, Dhumralochana was reduced to ashes. The demons were shocked to see their commander

dead in front of their eyes. "Let us surround her and attack," shouted one of the demons.

Ambika, mounted on her lion, looked at the demons and frowned. From her frown emerged Kali, the fiercest goddess. Her red tongue was coated with blood, and a garland of skulls adorned her neck. In one of her hands was a scimitar and in the other two were the chopped heads of demons.

Kali charged at the demons with all her fury. She pulled an elephant by the trunk and flung the elephant at the demons. "I will kill you with my bare hands," shouted Chanda and rushed towards her. Kali seized him by the hair and killed him.

She then charged at all the other demons with the same fury. The demons ran amok on the battlefield, unable to bear Kali's anger. Munda, who rushed towards her also met with the same fate as the other demons. He was killed fighting Kali.

"Kali! You have killed Chanda and Munda. From now on, another name for you will be Chamundi," said Goddess Ambika.

News reached Shumbha that Chanda and Munda had been killed. He rushed to the battlefield to avenge the defeat of the demons. The gods, who were witnessing this battle, sent forth powerful goddesses created by each one of them. From Brahma emerged Brahmani, who flew to the battle on her chariot of swans. From Vishnu, emerged Vaishnavi, who flew to the battle on a giant eagle.

From Mahesh (another name for Lord Shiva) emerged Maheshwari, who rode to the battle on a bull.

All the goddesses attacked the demons with great fury. Brahmani sprinkled sacred water from the heavens, which made the demons weak. One of the demons—Raktabeeja—was killed by one of the goddesses. As his blood touched the ground, hundreds of Raktabeejas sprung forth. Each time the goddesses killed the demons, more arose from their blood.

Goddess Durga knew that the only way to stop the demons from appearing was to turn to Kali for help. "Kali, you are our only saviour. Not a drop of their blood should touch the ground," said Durga. "I will ensure that not a drop touches the ground, and not one demon is created," said Kali. With Kali absorbing all their blood, the goddesses succeeded in killing hundreds of demons.

Nishumbha (Shumbha's brother), Raktabeeja and many other powerful demons were all killed by the goddesses. "Durga, your

victory is not yours alone. You have sought help from all the goddesses. Fight me alone and I will kill you," screamed Shumbha.

"If that is your desire, so be it," said Durga. All the goddesses merged into Durga. She flung her trident at Shumbha and killed him.

"Oh! Holy mother! You have restored peace once again. We salute you, Goddess Durga," said the gods.

And thus, the gods returned to where they belonged—Heaven.

Lakshmi

Indra was all set to be crowned as the King of the gods. At his crowning ceremony, all the gods and goddesses were present in complete splendour. "Indra, to win the heart of Shreedevi, the goddess of fortune, you will have to protect Bhoodevi, the goddess of Earth,"said someone. "I will gladly do so," replied Indra.

But, soon after he was crowned as the King, Indra lost interest in being a ruler. He took to drinking wine, and spent his time singing and dancing with the apsaras in Heaven.

"Indra has deserted us. There is no one to rule over Earth and Heaven," lamented the gods. The demons saw this as a great opportunity to loot Earth. They stole wealth from people's houses and created havoc in their lives.

Goddess Lakshmi saw what was happening and became very sad. "I will not be able to witness both, Earth and Heaven, going through such a turmoil," she thought to herself and dissolved herself into the ocean of milk.

Without Lakshmi, the gods and demons were left in panic. "How can we live without prosperity and wealth?" cried one of the demons. "We have to bring her back," said one of the gods. Lord Vishnu knew that the gods and demons had learnt their lesson.

"There is only one way to bring her back," he said. "What is it?" asked the gods. "Churn the ocean of milk," replied Vishnu.

Mandara, the king of mountains became the spindle. Akupara, the king of turtles became the base of the spindle. Vasuki, the king of serpents was the churning

rope. The gods and the demons began churning the ocean of milk. The churn twisted and turned, the ocean frothed and fumed, waves roared and spewed foam in every direction.

After months of churning the ocean, Goddess Lakshmi was pleased by the efforts of gods and demons. She emerged from the ocean in all her splendour.

"Oh goddess! We are blessed with your radiance," exclaimed the gods. Lakshmi was seated on a lotus, dressed in red silk. The sacred elephants that hold up the sky came from the eight quarters of the universe, raised their trunks and showered her with life-sustaining water.

"Who is the ugly one who walks by the side of Lakshmi?" asked a demon to the other. "She is my sister, Alakshmi," replied Lakshmi. "While I will dwell where there is nobility, righteousness,

virtue and clean surroundings, my sister will dwell where there is envy, greed, lust, pride and arrogance," she said.

Lakshmi garlanded Lord Vishnu who was present with a floral garland and thus became his bride.

Thus, Lord Vishnu is also known as Shree Natha (the husband of Shree, the goddess of fortune).

Goddess Lakshmi and Lord Vishnu returned to their abode, Vaikuntha.

Lakshmi and Virtue

Once upon a time, a demon king called Prahlada ruled the three worlds. He had made even Indra weak with his honesty and goodness.

"Oh master, is there any way I can get Heaven back from him?" Indra asked Brihaspati, the teacher of the gods. "As long as he has virtue with him, you cannot win over him," replied Brihaspati.

Indra decided that the only way to trick Prahlada was to ask him something in alms. So, he dressed up as a poor brahmin. He knew that Prahlada would never turn a brahmin away without giving him what he desired.

"My lord, I have come to you with a desire," said Indra in the guise of a brahmin to Prahlada. "And, what is that desire?" asked Prahlada. "Please gift me your virtue," said the brahmin. "Granted!" said Prahlada without thinking even for a moment. The brahmin went away smiling.

A few minutes later, Prahlada felt a sharp pain in his body. He saw a form coming out of his body. It looked like a man. "Who are you?" asked Prahlada.

"I am virtue, the one you just gifted," replied the form.

Prahlada looked in surprise as virtue flew out of the palace.

A little later, he felt pain again. "Who is it this time?" he asked. "I am righteousness," replied the form. "Where there is no virtue, I have no place," said the form and flew out of the palace.

Prahlada knew that he had given the brahmin more than what he had asked for. His silence was broken by another form. "I am honesty," said the form. "Where there is no righteousness, I have no place," said the form and disappeared. Within

seconds, another form came out of his body. “I am nobility. Where there is no virtue or righteousness, there can be no nobility,” said the form and left the palace.

Prahlada was seated at the foot of his throne—a defeated man. He heard the footsteps of a lady this time. He looked up and saw a dazzling figure. “Who are you and why are you leaving me?” he asked. “I am Goddess Lakshmi,

the goddess of fortune and prosperity," replied the lady. "I cannot reside where there is no virtue, righteousness, nobility and honesty,"she replied.

Prahlada knew that the brahmin was no ordinary one. He would have known that virtue was the most important quality to be asked for. "Tell me who that brahmin was," he asked the goddess. "It was Indra, the King of the gods," replied Goddess Lakshmi. "He knew what he had to take away from you to take all of us with him," said the goddess and left the palace.

Thus, fortune and prosperity lie in the place where there is honesty, nobility, virtue and righteousness.

Saraswati

Saraswati, the wife of Lord Brahma is known as the goddess of wisdom, art and music.

Goddess Saraswati is believed to bestow every human being with the power of speech, wisdom and learning. She has four hands representing the four aspects of human personality in learning: mind, intellect, alertness and ego. She has sacred scriptures in one hand and a lotus—the symbol of true knowledge—in the other. With her other two hands she plays the music of love and life on a stringed instrument called the Veena. She is dressed in white and rides a swan, both symbolising purity.

Kumbhakarna, the brother of the mighty Ravana, was a terror to sages. He was so big that he would torment all of them. Ravana was pleased with his brother, but Vibhishana was not. "It is not befitting a kshatriya to harm an innocent person," advised Vibhishana. But his advice always fell on deaf ears.

The sages were unable to bear his evil ways and went to Indra for help. "I will teach Kumbhakarna a lesson,"

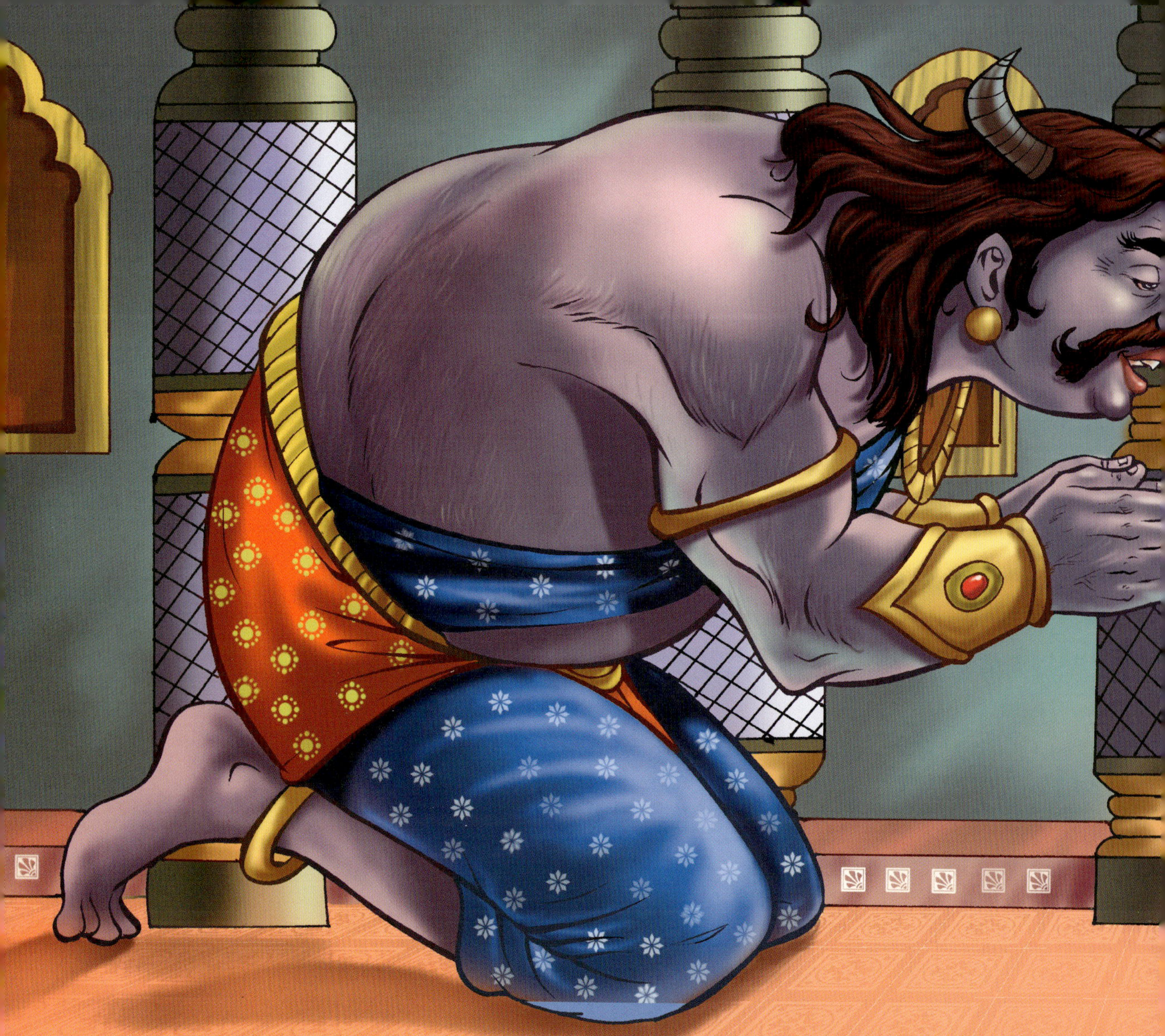

said Indra angrily and rode to Lanka with a huge army. He threw a blazing mace at Kumbhakarna who was waiting for him. Kumbhakarna swallowed the mace as if it was a sweet. He then caught hold of Airavat's (Indra's white elephant) trunk and toppled it.

Indra and his army fled from Lanka. When Ravana heard of what Kumbhakarna had done, he was immensely pleased. "You are the mightiest warrior Kumbhakarna," said Ravana in delight. "But we need to get more strength and power from Lord Brahma,"

said Ravana thoughtfully. "Let us meditate upon him," he said. All the three brothers went to the mountains and meditated upon Lord Brahma.

Lord Brahma appeared before Ravana and asked him what he desired. "I want to rule over the three worlds," asked Ravana. "So be it!" said Brahma. Indra knew that Kumbhakarna was next in line for the boon. "Kumbhakarna is already too strong," thought Indra. "If he gets more powers from Brahma, the three worlds will be doomed," he thought and rushed to Goddess Saraswati.

"Goddess, only you can save the three worlds from Kumbhakarna's evil ways," pleaded Indra. "Indra, I will help you by making him ask for a foolish boon," said Saraswati and flew to where Kumbhakarna was.

"Kumbhakarna, ask me what you desire," said Brahma. At that moment Saraswati controlled Kumbhakarna's speech. "I want a boon to sleep for all the twenty four hours,"
said Kumbhakarna. "So be it!" replied Brahma.

Ravana who heard his brother was in shock. "If he sleeps all the time, someone will kill him," he pleaded with Brahma. "In that case, he will sleep for six months at a time. Then he will stay awake for one whole day.

But if someone wakes him up in between, his life will be in danger," said Brahma and vanished.

Ravana returned to Lanka with his brothers, a sad man.

OTHER TITLES IN THIS SERIES